Hear the **honking** horn?
Feel the wind **blowing**
through the open windows?

You've seen cars from the outside. They come in many sizes, shapes
and colours. But what do cars look like beneath the bonnet?
Turn the page for a peek ...

WHAT'S BENEATH

PEEKING UNDER the BONNET

by Esther Porter   illustrated by Andrés Lozano

raintree
a Capstone comp

Cars are cool!

See the **shiny** wheels? Hear the engine **growl**?

A car has many parts. Some parts work together to start the car and make it move. Some parts stop it. Others keep the car and its passengers cool. Parts that work together make up a system. Motor technicians check car systems. They use computers to find problems.

If something is wrong, motor technicians try to fix it. They may need to install new parts.

Power up!

An engine gives a car power. Thousands of small explosions happen inside an engine every minute. The explosions move the car forwards. Each explosion happens inside a cylinder. Most cars have four to eight cylinders. The cylinders work together. They move pistons up and down. Pistons act like your legs pedalling a bike.

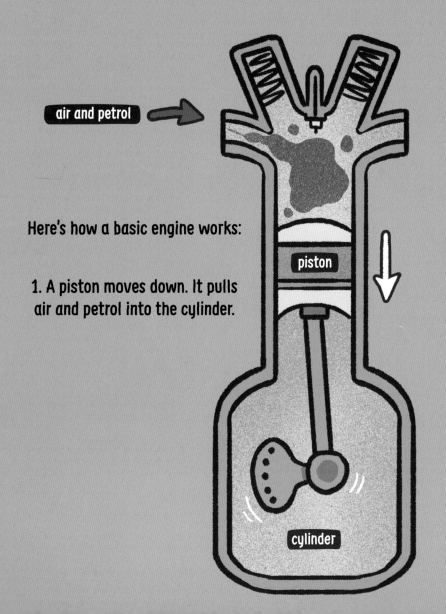

air and petrol

piston

cylinder

Here's how a basic engine works:

1. A piston moves down. It pulls air and petrol into the cylinder.

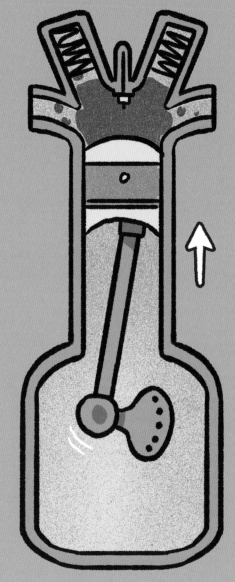

2. The piston moves up. It squeezes the air and petrol.

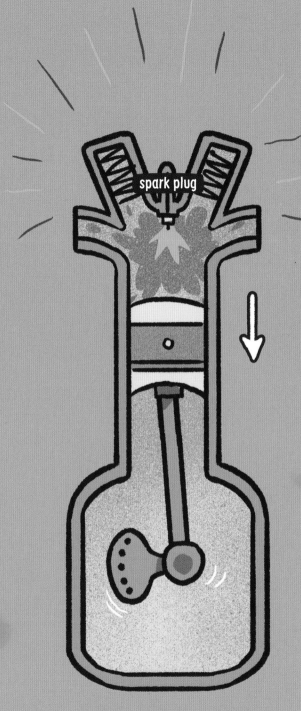

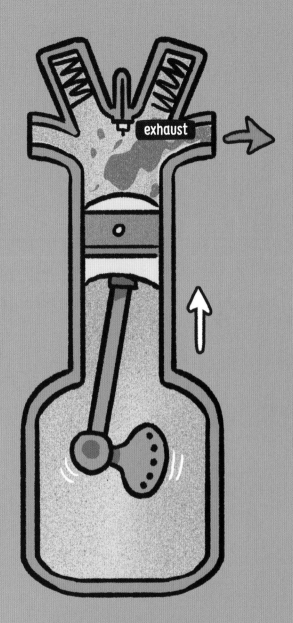

spark plug

exhaust

3. A spark plug ignites the squeezed air and petrol. BOOM!
The explosion pushes the piston back down again.

4. The piston moves back up. It pushes the exhaust from the cylinder.

Add the fuel

What powers the engine? Fuel! Next time you visit a petrol station, watch your parents. See how they add petrol or diesel to the car's fuel tank. When a car is running, a fuel pump sends petrol or diesel from the tank to the engine. Press the accelerator pedal, and air is sent to the engine too.

Exhaust is a mixture of used-up fuel and air. See how it leaves a car? It goes through the silencer and out of the exhaust pipe.

Keep cool

It gets hot under the bonnet!
A car engine needs to keep cool.
If it overheats it won't work. Oil
stops an engine from getting too
hot. Coolant also helps. It flows
through a hose and small holes
around the engine. The coolant
pulls away heat.

Time to move

How does the power in an engine move a car forwards? The transmission. Remember how the pistons move up and down like pedals on a bike? Your bike needs to change gears for more power. So does a car. The pistons need a set of gears to send more power to the wheels.

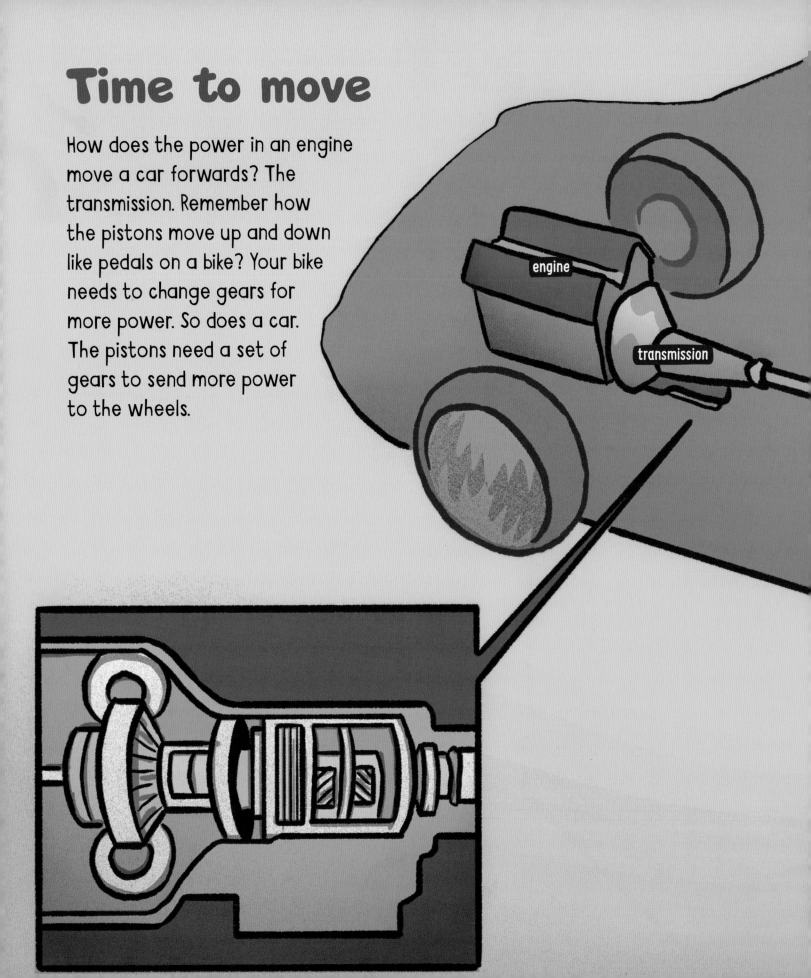

engine

transmission

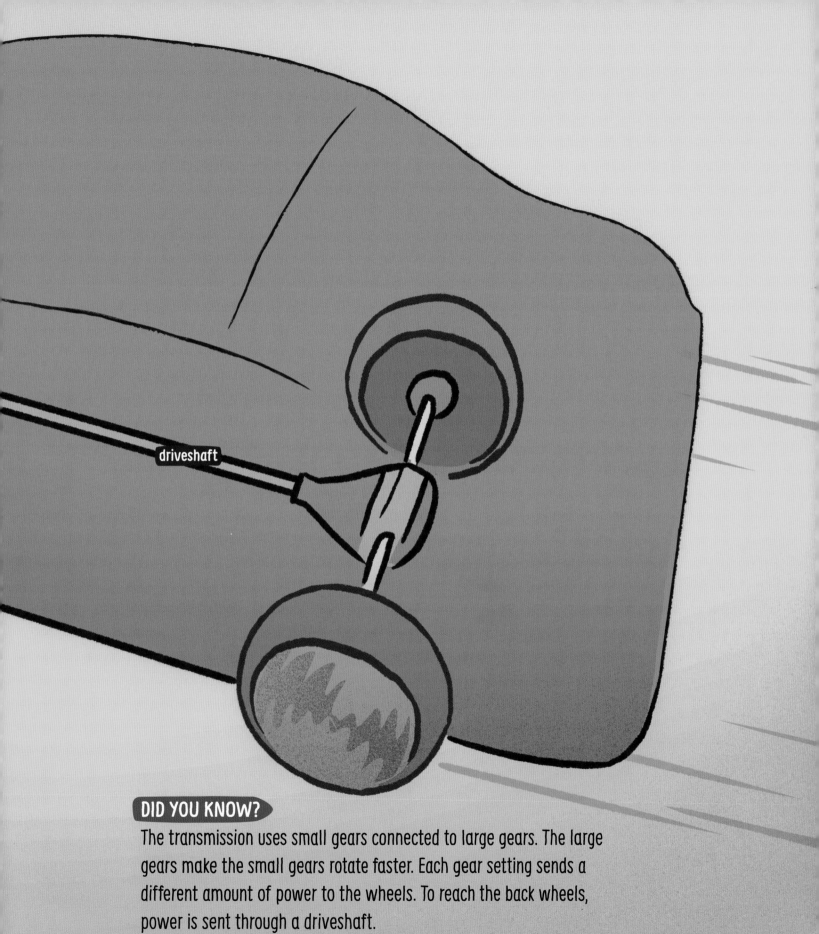

driveshaft

DID YOU KNOW?

The transmission uses small gears connected to large gears. The large gears make the small gears rotate faster. Each gear setting sends a different amount of power to the wheels. To reach the back wheels, power is sent through a driveshaft.

Flowing here, flowing there

Just like your body, a car needs lots of fluids. An engine needs oil to prevent overheating and to run smoothly. The transmission needs fluid too. Fluid allows the gears to change and keeps the gears in position. Cars also need brake fluid and power steering fluid.

brake fluid

DID YOU KNOW?
Unlike air, liquid does not compress (get smaller). So we use liquid to lock things into place. Transmission fluid locks gears. Brake fluid stops the wheels. Power steering fluid allows the steering wheel and tyres to turn.

Just a spark

What is the first thing your parents do to start the car? They turn the key in the ignition. Turning the key pulls power from the battery to start the car. The battery holds a car's electrical power. Once the car wakes up, the alternator takes over. The alternator is near the front of the engine.

battery

alternator

The alternator powers the headlights, brake lights and indicator lights. It powers the dashboard displays. It recharges the battery and runs the car's computer.

ignition switch

Think, think

Does a car have a brain? Yes! Sort of.

A computer acts like a car's brain. It makes sure the engine is getting enough power. It sets the transmission to the right gear. It makes sure the brakes are working. It controls the air temperature inside the car. The computer also triggers warning lights when something is wrong.

Hot and cold

Cars don't do well if they are too hot or too cold. Neither do their passengers! There are systems to keep people comfortable. If it's cold outside, a heater warms people. A fan blows air across the heater and into the car. **Toasty!**

When it's hot outside, an air conditioner cools people.

A car skeleton

What holds a car together? The chassis (rhymes with "lassie"). The chassis is like a car skeleton. All of a car's parts are attached to it.

The chassis gives a car its shape. The chassis holds a car's engine and suspension. The suspension absorbs the bumps in the road. It also prevents the car from bouncing, so you don't get carsick.

Stop!

Now you know what makes a car go. How does it stop? Think about the bike again. When you press the brake lever, pads press against the tyre. The tyre stops.

master cylinder (pistons)

brake pedal

Pressing the brake pedal in a car works much the same way. Brake fluid presses into pistons. The pistons make the brake pads squeeze the brake discs. The discs help slow and then stop the car's turning wheels.

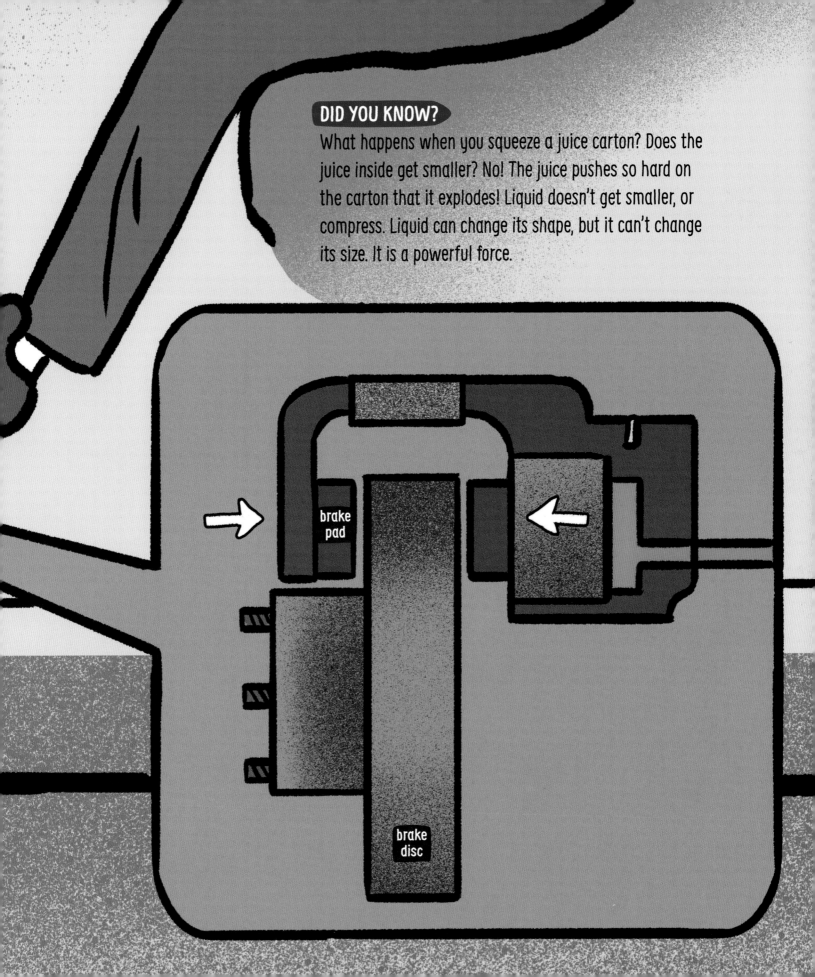

brake
pad

brake
disc

Rolling along

Tyres are the only parts of a car that touch the road. They're made of tough rubber. Tyres have grooves to help them grip the road. The grooves are called tread. Air-filled tyres help a car roll smoothly. When a car rolls smoothly, it uses less fuel. Why? A rough ride makes an engine work hard. The engine needs more power to move the car. More power means more fuel.

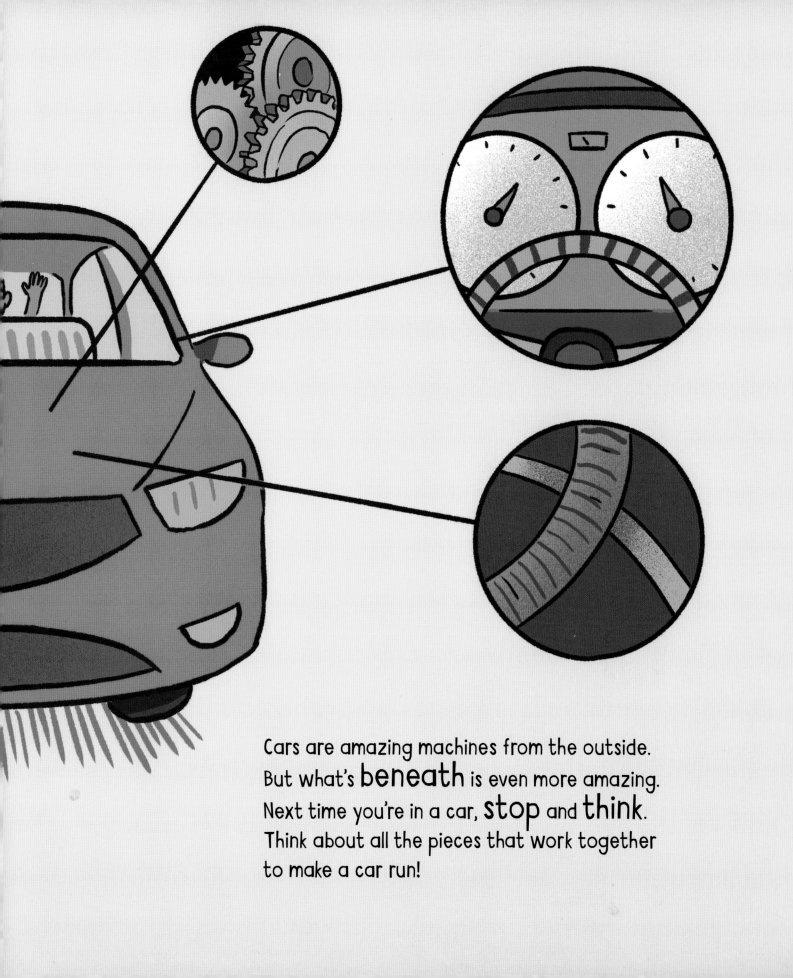

Cars are amazing machines from the outside.
But what's **beneath** is even more amazing.
Next time you're in a car, **stop** and **think**.
Think about all the pieces that work together
to make a car run!

GLOSSARY

absorb soak up

chassis frame or skeleton of a car

coolant mixture of water and antifreeze that flows through an engine and carries off heat

cylinder metal chamber; standard cars have four to eight cylinders in an engine

driveshaft part of a vehicle that carries power from the transmission gears to the wheels

engine machine that makes the power needed to move something

exhaust mixture of used-up fuel and air that comes out of a car's exhaust pipe

gear toothed wheel that fits into another toothed wheel

ignite cause something to burn

install put in

motor technician person who fixes vehicles or machinery; also called an engineer

piston part of an engine that moves up and down within a cylinder

rotate spin around

spark plug device that ignites the air and fuel inside an engine

suspension system of springs and shock absorbers that absorbs a car's up-and-down movements

transmission series of gears that sends power from the engine to the wheels

FIND OUT MORE
BOOKS

How Cars Work, Nick Arnold (Templar Publishing, 2012)

How Electric and Hybrid Cars Work (Eco Works), Louise Spilsbury (Franklin Watts, 2015)

How Machines Work: Fast Cars, Ian Graham (Franklin Watts, 2008)

WEBSITES

www.funkidslive.com/features/fun-kids-guide-to-cars/

Visit this site to find out more about how cars work.

www.blastscience.co.uk/ask-a-scientist/how-does-a-car-engine-work-when-you-put-petrol-in-it-what-makes-it-go-ella-age-8

An engineer explains to an 8-year-old girl how petrol makes a car go.

COMPREHENSION QUESTIONS

1. Look back at the images in the "Stop!" chapter. Describe how the braking system stops a car.

2. The suspension is what keeps a car from bouncing over bumps in the road. What do you think it would be like to drive over a gravel road without suspension?

3. What do motor technicians do? Why are they important?

Raintree is an imprint of Capstone Global Library Limited, a company incorporated in England and Wales having its registered office at 264 Banbury Road, Oxford, OX2 7DY – Registered company number: 6695582

www.raintree.co.uk
myorders@raintree.co.uk

ISBN 978 1 4747 1305 4 (hardback)
19 18 17 16 15
10 9 8 7 6 5 4 3 2 1

ISBN 978 1 4747 1309 2 (paperback)
20 19 18 17 16
10 9 8 7 6 5 4 3 2 1

British Library Cataloguing in Publication Data
A full catalogue record for this book is available from the British Library.

Editorial Credits
Jill Kalz, editor; Russell Griesmer, designer; Nathan Gassman, creative director; Katy LaVigne, production specialist

Acknowledgements
We would like to thank Sheldon Newkirk, Automotive Instructor, Blackhawk Technical College, USA, for his invaluable help in the preparation of this book.

Every effort has been made to contact copyright holders of material reproduced in this book. Any omissions will be rectified in subsequent printings if notice is given to the publisher.

All the Internet addresses (URLs) given in this book were valid at the time of going to press. However, due to the dynamic nature of the Internet, some addresses may have changed, or sites may have changed or ceased to exist since publication. While the author and publisher regret any inconvenience this may cause readers, no responsibility for any such changes can be accepted by either the author or the publisher.

Printed and bound in China.

LOOK FOR ALL THE BOOKS IN THE SERIES:

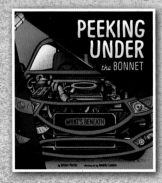
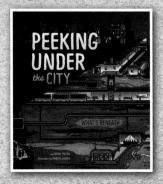
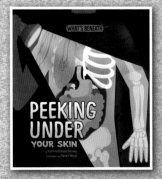